Clucky

Story and illustrations
by Elizabeth Russell-Arnot

Clucky and her nine little yellow chicks were walking around the farm.

Clucky was looking for food to give her babies.

She looked in the grass and she looked under the stones.

3

Clucky didn't see a big rat
hiding under the hen house.
It was watching Clucky
and her nine little chicks.

The rat wanted to catch
a chick to eat.

Clucky always tried
to keep her babies with her.
But it was very hard to watch them
all the time.

One little chick saw a worm
by the long grass
and ran to get it.

Clucky didn't see the little chick
run over to the worm.

But the farm cat,
who was sitting on the fence,
saw the little chick.

The cat was just going to jump down
and get the little chick,
when the rat ran out
from under the hen house.

The rat had seen the little chick, too.

The cat jumped down
from the fence.
But he didn't try to get the chick.
He wanted to get the rat.
The rat was bigger,
and it would be much better to eat.

The cat raced after the rat.

Clucky turned around.
She saw the cat
running after the rat.

"Cluck! Cluck!" she called
to her naughty little yellow chick.
"Cluck! Cluck! Cluck!"

The little chick got the worm
and ran back to Clucky.

Clucky opened her wings,
and all the little yellow chicks
ran to her.

She sat down
with the little chicks
under her wings.
Now they would be safe
from the cats and rats
on the farm.